Implementing AppFog

An effective, hands-on guide on deploying applications
to the cloud using the AppFog service

Matthew Nohr

Isaac Rabinovitch

BIRMINGHAM - MUMBAI

Implementing AppFog

First published: November 2012

Production Reference: 1121113

Published by Packt Publishing Ltd.
Livery Place
35 Livery Street
Birmingham B3 2PB, UK.

ISBN 978-1-84969-818-4

www.packtpub.com

Cover Image by Prashant Timappa Shetty (sparkling.spectrum.123@gmail.com)

Credits

Authors
Matthew Nohr

Isaac Rabinovitch

Reviewers
Ngo The Hung

Abhilash Nanda

Tom O'Connor

Acquisition Editor
Nikhil Karkal

Commissioning Editor
Manasi Pandire

Technical Editors
Dipika Gaonkar

Gauri Dasgupta

Project Coordinator
Joel Goveya

Proofreader
Amy Johnson

Indexer
Mariammal Chettiyar

Production Coordinator
Shantanu Zagade

Cover Work
Shantanu Zagade

About the Authors

Matthew Nohr is a software developer with over ten years of experience in creating large scale applications. He has worked on a range of projects from enterprise Java desktop applications to commercial Java server-based products to cloud-based Groovy/Grails services. Matthew is a certified Scrum Master and has a Masters degree in Software Engineering.

> I'd like to thank my wife Katie for supporting me though yet another one of my diversions.

Isaac Rabinovitch is a freelance technical writer in Portland, Oregon. He's worked with computers since the days they filled whole rooms and had hundreds of blinking lights. He's written documentation for programmers, system administrators, data center personnel, and ordinary people. His former employees include Sun, SGI, Borland, and Zilog. He's the co-author of the *Java Tutorial, 4th edition*. Read more about him at `picknit.com`.

> I want to thank many folks at Portland hackathons, meetups, and other venues for their help and support. Their spirit is something that makes PDX is a great place to work on technology.

About the Reviewers

Ngo The Hung is a passionate software developer who loves open source technologies and frameworks. He is not afraid to get his hands dirty and his feet wet, he is open to most technologies as long as they are useful and fun. He also has experience in mobile development and web technologies, he has worked with multiple mobile platforms (Android/iPhone/Windows 8), open source portals, frameworks, and content management systems. In his free time, he reads manga and watches movies.

If you love to work with him or just have a talk, visit him at `http://ngo-hung.com` or drop him a note at `thehung111@gmail.com`.

Abhilash Nanda has completed a Masters in CSE from IIT Hyderabad. He has two years experience in commercial development and a total of five years in programming. Currently he works as a software developer at TopTalent.in. He loves to learn new technologies and programming patterns that reduce human effort.

An enthusiastic programmer, writer, and thinker. When strolling alone, he thinks about the world or else about some architecture to be implemented. He loves to play cricket and has a heartfelt connection to novels and poetry.

> I would like to thank every single person who has come into and out of my life, for the way they have shaped me into who I am.

Tom O'Connor is an experienced systems architect and DevOps engineer, living in the West Midlands in the United Kingdom. Over the last eight years, he has worked in a wide variety of companies, from e-commerce, to video effects, and now owns his own company providing systems consultancy for wireless network design and installations.

Tom writes a technical blog on his website, providing both tutorial articles, and updates on what he's been working on. He has wide reaching skills and experience gathered over the last ten years, having worked on Windows, Linux, and Unix systems for most of that time, coupled with recent experience in designing and building high-performance computer systems.

He is also an active member of the UK DevOps community, as well as a Community Moderator on `ServerFault.com`, where he demonstrates his expertise and skills to a wide audience.

Tom also worked on reviewing *Learning AWS OpsWorks*, which was published in September 2013.

www.PacktPub.com

Support files, eBooks, discount offers and more

You might want to visit www.PacktPub.com for support files and downloads related to your book.

Did you know that Packt offers eBook versions of every book published, with PDF and ePub files available? You can upgrade to the eBook version at www.PacktPub.com and as a print book customer, you are entitled to a discount on the eBook copy. Get in touch with us at service@packtpub.com for more details.

At www.PacktPub.com, you can also read a collection of free technical articles, sign up for a range of free newsletters and receive exclusive discounts and offers on Packt books and eBooks.

http://PacktLib.PacktPub.com

Do you need instant solutions to your IT questions? PacktLib is Packt's online digital book library. Here, you can access, read and search across Packt's entire library of books.

Why Subscribe?

- Fully searchable across every book published by Packt
- Copy and paste, print and bookmark content
- On demand and accessible via web browser

Free Access for Packt account holders

If you have an account with Packt at www.PacktPub.com, you can use this to access PacktLib today and view nine entirely free books. Simply use your login credentials for immediate access.

Table of Contents

Preface

AppFog is a cloud-based solution that allows users to quickly build and deploy applications without having to handle server configuration and setup. This book is intended to help you to quickly get started using AppFog and learn to create and deploy applications to the AppFog cloud.

What this book covers

Chapter 1, Getting Started With AppFog, creates an account with AppFog and gets your first application running.

Chapter 2, Using the Command-line Tool, installs and uses the command line tool to download an application from AppFog, then modifies and uploads it back to the cloud.

Chapter 3, Using Databases, uses AppFog's backend services to create a data store for your application.

Chapter 4, Creating an Application From Scratch, creates an application using only the command line tools and gets it running in the cloud.

Chapter 5, Command-line Reference, helps you learn about the many command line tools available.

Appendix, Installing the AppFog Gem, helps you install the Ruby Gem to be able to use the command line tools.

What you need for this book

The examples in the book are written in Ruby and HTML. To follow along you will need to have Ruby running on your computer. You will have to install the AppFog Ruby Gem, which is explained in the book.

Who this book is for

This book is aimed at anyone who wants to deploy applications to the cloud using AppFog. It is written mainly for developers who are writing their own applications to deploy.

Conventions

In this book, you will find a number of styles of text that distinguish between different kinds of information. Here are some examples of these styles, and an explanation of their meaning.

A block of code is set as follows:

```
require 'sinatra'

get '/' do
  "Inside AppFog"
end
```

Any command-line input or output is written as follows:

```
$ af pull insideaf1
```

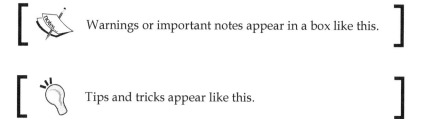

Warnings or important notes appear in a box like this.

Tips and tricks appear like this.

Reader feedback

Feedback from our readers is always welcome. Let us know what you think about this book—what you liked or may have disliked. Reader feedback is important for us to develop titles that you really get the most out of.

To send us general feedback, simply send an e-mail to feedback@packtpub.com, and mention the book title through the subject of your message.

If there is a topic that you have expertise in and you are interested in either writing or contributing to a book, see our author guide on www.packtpub.com/authors.

Customer support

Now that you are the proud owner of a Packt book, we have a number of things to help you to get the most from your purchase.

Downloading the example code

You can download the example code files for all Packt books you have purchased from your account at http://www.packtpub.com. If you purchased this book elsewhere, you can visit http://www.packtpub.com/support and register to have the files e-mailed directly to you.

Errata

Although we have taken every care to ensure the accuracy of our content, mistakes do happen. If you find a mistake in one of our books—maybe a mistake in the text or the code—we would be grateful if you would report this to us. By doing so, you can save other readers from frustration and help us improve subsequent versions of this book. If you find any errata, please report them by visiting http://www.packtpub.com/support, selecting your book, clicking on the **errata submission form** link, and entering the details of your errata. Once your errata are verified, your submission will be accepted and the errata will be uploaded to our website, or added to any list of existing errata, under the Errata section of that title.

Piracy

Piracy of copyright material on the Internet is an ongoing problem across all media. At Packt, we take the protection of our copyright and licenses very seriously. If you come across any illegal copies of our works, in any form, on the Internet, please provide us with the location address or website name immediately so that we can pursue a remedy.

Please contact us at copyright@packtpub.com with a link to the suspected pirated material.

We appreciate your help in protecting our authors, and our ability to bring you valuable content.

Questions

You can contact us at questions@packtpub.com if you are having a problem with any aspect of the book, and we will do our best to address it.

Getting Started with AppFog

1

You can create an AppFog account and have your first application up and running in minutes. This chapter shows you how to perform this, and also demonstrates some of the features of the application control panel.

 You can create and deploy several applications using AppFog's free service level, which allows you to use up to 2 GB of RAM. You can use the free service level without supplying a credit card number. Some advanced features, such as use of external domain names, SSL, and team access, are only available to the paid users.

About AppFog

AppFog is a platform that you can use to host and deploy your applications to the cloud. You can write applications in Java, Node.js, Ruby, Python, or PHP and it also has built-in support for MySQL, PostgreSQL, MongoDB, Redis, and RabbitMQ. Applications and their services can all be configured from a simple dashboard in a matter of minutes. AppFog also provides scalable architectures with load balancing so as your applications grow, you can easily increase the number of instances you have running.

There are free and paid plans. The paid plans currently start at $20 and go up from there depending on how much memory, storage, and instances you need. There are also enterprise level plans for larger businesses.

One of the main benefits of using AppFog is that it reduces the amount of time you need to spend on configuring servers, installing and configuring firewalls and security, and managing load balancers.

Creating an account

Create an AppFog account using the following steps:

1. Go to www.appfog.com and click on **Sign Up**.

2. The **Create an account** form appears. Fill it in and click on **Signup**.

3. After clicking on **Signup**, you will need to verify your e-mail. Once activated, you will be taken to your profile page.

4. On your profile page, click on **Create App**. This will take you to the new apps page. We will cover this page in the next section.

Creating and deploying a preconfigured application

The new apps page helps you create and deploy a preconfigured application. Applications can be in one of several programming languages, including Ruby, Python, Java, PHP, and Node.js. These languages can be used with various application frameworks and backend services. In this chapter, you will create and deploy a basic "Hello World" application written in the Ruby programming language and utilizing the Sinatra application framework. No knowledge of Ruby or Sinatra is needed for this initial step.

1. Go to the New Apps page. If you've just created your account, you will go to the profile page and can then click on **New App**. Otherwise, go to `console.appfog.com` and click on **create app**.

2. Choose an application platform. The first section of the **New Apps** page is a list of platforms labeled **Step 1: Choose an application**. Your first application will run on Ruby and Sinatra, so click that icon.

3. Choose an infrastructure. This is the cloud hosting provider that will run your application. For this simple application, you can choose any infrastructure that supports Ruby. You will see a red exclamation mark on any infrastructures that do not support your selected application. Have look at the following screenshot for reference:

 Buttons for infrastructures that support Ruby have **RUBY** in a white-on-gray rectangle. Infrastructures that do not support Ruby will have a red exclamation mark.

4. Choose an application name. This name will form part of a URL you can use to access your application in a Web browser. Click on **Create App**, as in the following screenshot:

- The web form refers to the application name as a "domain" or a "subdomain" because it's part of a web site URL. You'll mainly use this name to identity the application to the command-line tool, so this book calls it the "application name".
- You can assign additional domain names to the application after you deploy it.

5. After you click on **Create App**, you go to a page that describes the progress of the application towards creation, staging, and running. Once it is running, you can click on the **Your App is ready** link to see it:

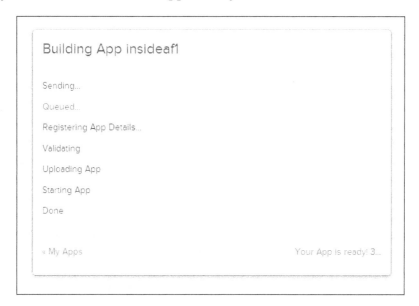

Using the application control panel

After you create an application, its control panel appears automatically. To access it otherwise perform the following steps:

1. Go to `console.appfog.com`. A list of applications appears:

2. Click on the application name in the left column. The application control panel appears:

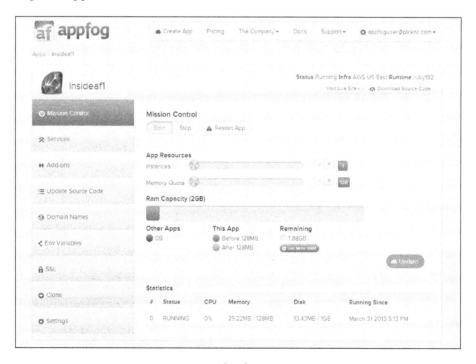

This console has many features, which we will explore in later chapters. For now, let's focus on just two features, which are listed in the following bullet list:

- If you click on the **Visit Live Site** button (upper-right), you go to your application, which is already running.

- If you click on **Domain Names** (left-side) you can assign additional domain names for application access. To support external domain names (such as mysite.com), you must upgrade your AppFog account to a paid level. The domain name itself is managed by a registrar, which is separate from AppFog.

To create a domain name, visit the website for a domain name registrar. You will need the A Record and CNAME Record data for the infrastructure you are using. This data is available on AppFog domain names screen. You can read AppFog help guide on custom domain names for more details.

Summary

In this chapter we learned how to:

- Create an AppFog account
- Create a preconfigured AppFog application
- Deploy the application and see it running
- Use AppFog control panel

In *Chapter 2, Using the Command-line Tool*, we are going to use AppFog command-line tool to download the application we created here, update it, and then redeploy it to AppFog.

2
Using the Command-line Tool

In this chapter, we'll learn how to install and use the AppFog command-line tool. We'll use this tool to download the application we created in first chapter. We'll run this application locally, modify it, test it, and send it back to the cloud infrastructure.

When you complete this chapter, you'll understand the complete AppFog application lifecycle.

Installing the AppFog Gem

The AppFog command-line tool is packaged as a Ruby software package, known as a "Gem". If you are already using Ruby, simply install the Gem named `af`.

If you're not familiar with Ruby, refer to *Appendix A*, which contains instructions for installing Ruby and the AppFog Gem on common platforms.

To verify that the Gem is installed, enter the following command:

```
$ af version
af 0.3.16.5
```

You will see `af` followed by your version number. See *Chapter 5, Command-line Reference* for details on all the command-line options.

Logging in

Before you can access cloud resources, you have to log in by entering the following command:

```
$ af login
```

You will be prompted for the e-mail address and password you used to create the account. If you correctly entered your credentials, you will see the following:

```
Successfully logged into [https://api/appfog.com]
```

To check your login status, type the following command and you will see your e-mail address:

```
$ af user
```

Getting application statuses

Once logged in, you can check the status of applications you previously deployed:

```
$ af apps
+-------------+----+---------+--------------------+----------+-----+
| Application | #  | Health  | URLS               | Services | In  |
+-------------+----+---------+--------------------+----------+-----+
| insideaf1   | 1  | RUNNING | insideaf1.aws.af.cm |         | aws |
+-------------+----+---------+--------------------+----------+-----+
```

These fields correspond to information on the web control panel. Note that the application name is the same as the "domain name" you used to create the application. This is the name you'll use to manage the application from the command line.

Downloading the application

Use the `pull` command to download a deployed application, as shown in the following command:

```
$ af pull insideaf1
Pulling last pushed source code: OK
```

The application is downloaded to a local directory whose name is the same as the application name – in this case, `insideaf1`.

Fixing the application for Ruby 1.8.7

If you're using Ruby 1.9.2 or later, you can run the application unchanged; you can skip this section. To check which version of Ruby you are using, you can type:

```
$ ruby -v
```

If you're using Ruby 1.8.7, you'll have to modify the program. The problem is the main application source file `app.rb`. Here's the program as AppFog provides it:

```
require 'sinatra'
set :protection, except: :ip_spoofing

get '/' do
  erb :index
end
```

There are two problems with this code. They are as follows:

- In Ruby 1.8.7, you have to explicitly indicate that you're using Gems. This is not necessary in later versions.

- The set line is a workaround for a bug in the AppFog software. This bug has long since been fixed, but the set command does no harm in later versions of Ruby. However, it is syntactically incorrect in Ruby 1.8.7 so you should remove that line.

Edit the source code so it looks like this:

```
require 'rubygems'
require 'sinatra'

get '/' do
  erb :index
end
```

Obviously, inconsistencies such as these between Ruby on your local system and Ruby on the AppFog infrastructures are unacceptable for serious application development. Since this book is using only Ruby to illustrate the development cycle, we don't deal with this issue. See *Appendix A* for more information.

Running the application

The application requires the Sinatra Gem to run. If you don't know how to install this Gem, refer to *Appendix A*.

Go to the directory containing the application and use the Ruby command to run the main source file.

```
$ cd insideaf1
$ ruby app.rb
[2013-04-18 13:59:22] INFO  WEBrick 1.3.1
[2013-04-18 13:59:22] INFO  ruby 1.9.3 (2012-04-20) [i686-linux]
== Sinatra/1.4.2 has taken the stage on 4567 for development with backup
from WEBrick
[2013-04-18 13:59:22] INFO  WEBrick::HTTPServer#start: pid=11048
port=4567
```

Now send your browser to `http://localhost:4567/`. The same application page you saw in *Chapter 1, Getting started with Appfog* appears. This time the application is running on your system instead of running on the cloud infrastructure.

To terminate the application, return to the command line and press *Ctrl + C*.

```
^C
== Sinatra has ended his set (crowd applauds)
[2013-04-18 14:51:49] INFO  going to shutdown ...
[2013-04-18 14:51:49] INFO  WEBrick::HTTPServer#start done.
```

Modifying the application

We're going to change the application slightly. Instead of displaying a simple message, we're going to display a list of environment variables and their values. Here's the Ruby program that does this on the command line:

```
ENV.each do |name, value|
  value = value[0..19] + "..." if value.length > 20
  print "#{name} = #{value}\n"
end
```

This is a simple loop that iterates through the name/value pairs in the program's environment. Many environment variable values are extremely long, so we truncate those that are longer than 20 characters.

In the Sinatra version of the application, the same logic is divided between the following two files:

- `app.rb`, which contains the main Ruby source code.
- `views/index.erb`, the ERB module that generates the page HTML.

Here's `app.rb` as provided by AppFog:

```
require 'sinatra'
set :protection, except: :ip_spoofing

get '/' do
  erb :index
end
```

The code we care about is contained in the last three lines. This specifies that an HTTP request to GET "/" causes the ERB module in `views/index.erb` be called. Normally, code like this passes information to the ERB module—and that's the change we make in our version:

```
get '/' do
  @env = ENV
  erb :index
end
```

The extra line sets an "instance variable" called `@env`. We won't talk about instance variables except to point out that they're visible to ERB modules. Thus this simple assignment makes the values in ENV accessible to the ERB module `index.erb`.

An ERB module is essentially an HTML page with embedded Ruby. We're going to discard the entire contents of `views/index.erb` and replace them with the following page definition:

```
<html><head>
  <title>Environment Variables</title>
</head><body>
  <h1>Environment Variables</h1>
  <table border="1" cellpadding="5">
    <tr>
      <td>Name</td>
      <td>Value</td>
    </tr>
    <% @env.each do |name, value| %>
      <% value = value[0..19] + "..." if value.length > 20 %>
      <tr>
        <td><%= name %></td>
        <td><%= value %></td>
      </tr>
    <% end %>
  </table>
</body>
</html>
```

Downloading the example code

You can download the example code files for all Packt books you have purchased from your account at http://www.packtpub.com. If you purchased this book elsewhere, you can visit http://www.packtpub.com/support and register to have the files e-mailed directly to you.

Most of this file is familiar HTML. Here are the embedded Ruby code lines and their functions:

```
<% @env.each do |name, value| %>
...
<% end %>
```

This defines the iteration loop for the values in `@env`. Any HTML within the loop is expanded once, each time the loop executes. Thus we get a table row for each environment variable:

```
<% value = value[0..19] + "..." if value.length > 20 %>
```

This truncates values longer than 20 characters:

```
<tr>
  <td><%= name %></td>
  <td><%= value %></td>
</tr>
```

This expands into a table row containing the values of `name` and `value`. Notice the use of the `=` character to indicate expansion of Ruby expressions.

Save these files and run them as before. Now when you point your browser at http://localhost:4567/, you get a listing of your applications environment:

Environment Variables

Name	Value
SSH_AGENT_PID	1290
GPG_AGENT_INFO	/run/user/isaac/keyr...
TERM	xterm
SHELL	/bin/bash
XDG_SESSION_COOKIE	13df8cb2a1e0f68b3aea...
WINDOWID	77594630
GNOME_KEYRING_CONTROL	/run/user/isaac/keyr...

Updating the running application

Once you have tested the local copy of your application, you're ready to update the copy running on the AppFog infrastructure, as follows:

```
$ af update insideaf1
Uploading Application:
  Checking for available resources: OK
  Packing application: OK
  Uploading (28K): OK
Push Status: OK
Stopping Application 'insideaf1': OK
Staging Application 'insideaf1': OK
Starting Application 'insideaf1': OK
```

Summary

In this chapter we:

- Installed the AppFog command-line tools
- Downloaded the application from AppFog
- Modified the application and uploaded it back to AppFog

In the next chapter we will create an application that uses AppFog's built-in services to set up a database.

3
Configuring Services

The AppFog services are preconfigured backend services you can use with your applications. These include data stores and message queues.

In this chapter we will set up a simple database using AppFog's MySQL service. To do this, we will create a new application, set up a database service through AppFog, create a database with sample data, and hook it all together.

Creating a database console application

Before you can create a service, you have to create an application that uses the service. If you're working with databases, one application that is convenient is a database console. The AppFog provides just what we need as a preconfigured application, so that's what we'll use. To do this, we'll use the AppFog console, just as we did in *Chapter 1*, *Getting Started with AppFog*. Perform the following steps for the same:

1. Point your browser at the AppFog console at `https://console.appfog.com`.
2. Click on **Create App** at the top of the page. The New Apps page appears.
3. Click on the button for **phpMyAdmin**.

4. Click on one of the supported infrastructure buttons, like in *Chapter 1, Getting Started with AppFog*.

5. Enter an application name under **Choose a subdomain**. For this example, I am going to use insideaf-admin as the name.

6. Click on **Create App**. After a delay while the application is created, the application control panel appears.

Before we can start to work with this application, we need to configure it and bind a database service to it. These are tasks we'll cover in the next two sections.

Configuring the database console

Most of the configuration for the database console has already been done. The one thing we need to provide is a password for the database administrator. (By default, the database administrator user name is the e-mail address you use as an AppFog user name.) Passwords are sensitive information and should never be included in application source code. Thus the console application doesn't store a password in its own files. Instead it looks for the password in an environment variable named **PMA_PASSWORD**. To set this variable:

1. If your web browser isn't already showing the application control panel, go to the AppFog console and click on the application name.

2. Click on the **Env Variables** button on the left side of the page.

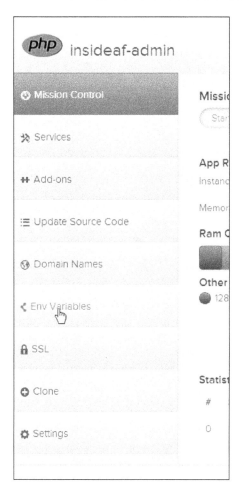

3. The environment variables display appears. Enter PMA_PASSWORD under **Name** and a password under **Value**.

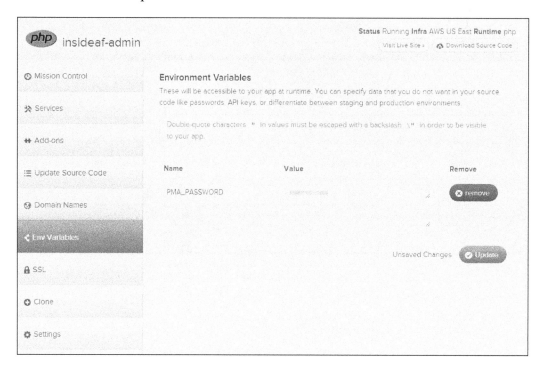

4. Click on **Update** to save the variable and restart the application.

 Creating or modifying environment variables always causes your application to restart so it can read the new values.

Creating and attaching a MySQL service

1. If your web browser isn't already showing the application control panel, go to the AppFog console and click on the application name.

2. Click on the **Services** button on the left side of the page. The **Services** display appears, as shown in the following screenshot:

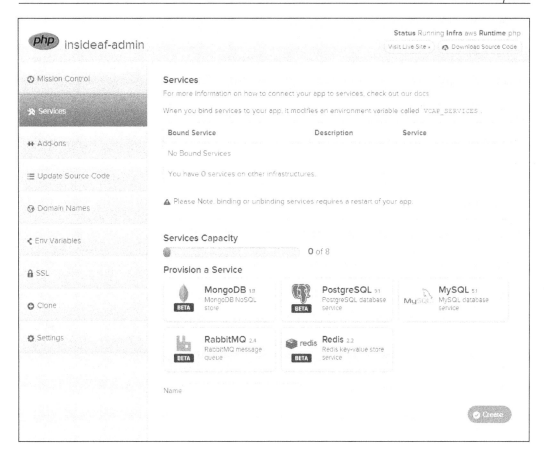

3. Under **Provision a Service**, click on the **MySQL** button.

4.   Enter a name for the service and click on the **Create** button.

After a short delay, the new service appears on the list of services bound to the application. This means that the service is ready and the application has been restarted. The database console is now ready for use.

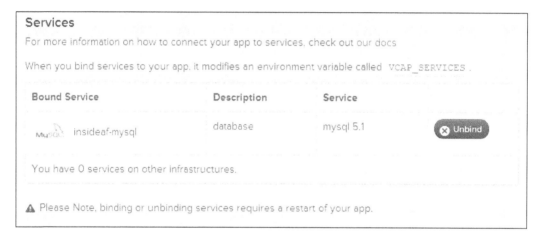

Creating and populating a database table

With the database console application active, you can open it in your web browser and use it to manipulate the MySQL service. We'll use the console application to create a database table and populate it. The table will implement a very simple to-do list.

Our database table will be called "Tasks" and will have three columns:

*   ID: It is an automatically incrementing number that uniquely identifies the row
*   Name: It is a string value containing the name of a task to be done
*   Completed: It is a Boolean value containing the completion status of the task.

Now, perform the following steps:

1. Point your web browser to the home page for the database console. If you didn't note the address when you created it, go to the application control panel and click on **Visit Live Site**.

2. An authentication dialog appears. The user name is the same e-mail address you use to access your AppFog account. The password is the value you previously set in the **PMA_PASSWORD** environment variable. Enter these and click on **Log In**. Refer the following screenshot:

3. The database console screen appears. Click on the **Create table** button on the left.

4. A table structure page appears. This page contains many fields that you can safely ignore. Enter the following:
   ○ At the top of the page under **Table name** enter **Tasks**
   ○ In the first row of the structure table, enter the following details:
   ○ Under **Name** enter ID

- ○ Under **Type** select INT
- ○ Under **A_I** (autoincrement) be sure the checkbox is checked
- ○ In the second row of the structure table, enter the following details:
- ○ Under **Name** enter Name
- ○ Under **Type** select VARCHAR
- ○ Under **Length/Value** enter 30
- ○ In the third row of the Structure table:
- ○ Under **Name** enter Completed
- ○ Under **Type** select Boolean

5. Click on the **Save** button in the lower right. The main application window reappears.

6. The name of the new table now appears on the left. Click on it.

7. A display for the new table appears. Notice that the type listed for the `Completed` column is `tinyint(1)`. In MySQL this type is used for Boolean values. Click on the **Insert** button at the top of the display as shown in the following screenshot:

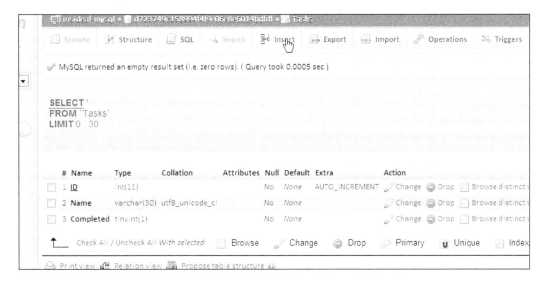

8. A form for entering database values appears. Under the **Value** column:
   ◦ Leave the `ID` value blank
   ◦ For `Name` enter `Create database table`
   ◦ For `Completed` enter `1`

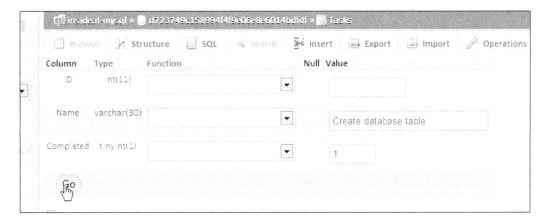

9. Click on the **Go** button.

You now have a database table populated with a single row of data.

Binding a service to an application

Now that we have a service, let's create an application that uses it. As a starting point, we'll use the application we created in *Chapter 2, Using the Command-line Tool*, which displays environment variables. Now, perform the following steps:

1. Go to the control panel page for the previous application.
2. Click on the **Clone** button on the left side. The **Clone Your App** display appears.
3. Choose an infrastructure. This must be the same infrastructure you chose for the database service.
4. Enter an application name under **Enter a domain**. For this example, I will use insideaf2 as the application name.

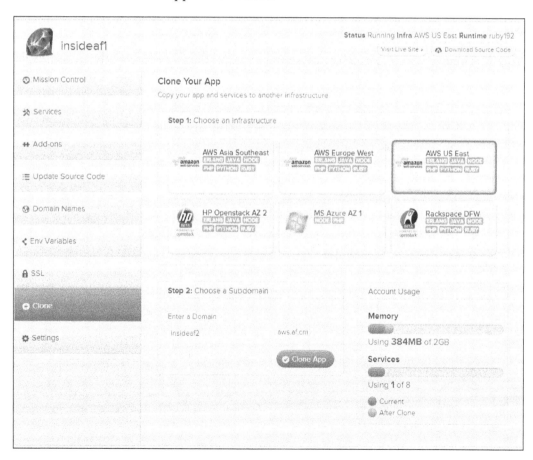

5. Click on the **Clone App** button. The control panel for the old application is replaced by a status display for the cloning process. Once the new application is up and running, its control panel appears.

6. Click on the **Services** button on the left side of the page. The services display appears. Notice that the **Bound Service** list is empty but that the **Other Services** list contains the database service you created.

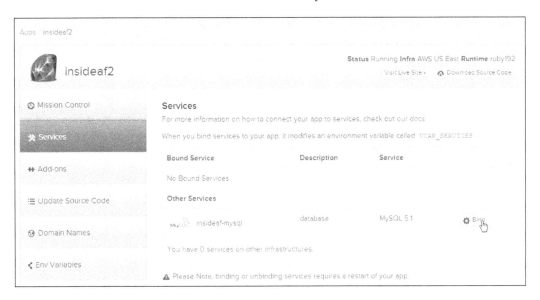

7. Click on the **Bind** button for the database service. There is a delay while your application is restarted. Once the process is complete, the database service appears in the **Bound Service** list.

8. Click on the **View Live Site** button at the top of the display. Notice that the application's environment variable list now includes VCAP_SERVICES. We'll use the contents of this variable to access the service from the application. Refer the following screenshot:

VCAP_DEBUG_IP		
VCAP_SERVICES	{"mysql-5.1":[{"name...	
VMC_WARNING_WARNING	All VMC_* environmen...	
VMC ADD VERSION	0.0b.d202216125f05d.	

Using the database in the application

Let's modify the application so that, instead of listing environment variables, its lists rows in the database. First we need to download the files for the new application, then use following command:

```
$ af pull insideaf2
$ cd insideaf2
```

The structure of the two applications is the same; we'll look at the low-level changes one-by-one. We make changes to the two files we looked at before, app.rb and views/index.erb. We also need to change Gem file.

Making changes to app.rb

First, let's go to app.rb and look at our list of required Gems:

```
require 'sinatra'
```

We're going to need two additional Gems, which are as follows:

- json: We'll use it to convert the JSON text in VCAP_SERVICES into a data structure
- mysql2: We'll use it to access the MySQL database

The expanded Gem requirements are as follows:

```
require 'sinatra'
require 'json'
require 'mysql2'
```

At the beginning of the application, we add new code that extracts MySQL credentials from the VCAP_SERVICES. This environment variable contains a JSON string that parses into a data structure similar to this example:

```
{
  "mysql-5.1"=>[
    {
      "name"=>"insideaf-mysql",
      "label"=>"mysql-5.1",
      "plan"=>"free",
      "tags"=>["mysql", "mysql-5.1", "relational", "mysql-5.1",
        "mysql"],
      "credentials"=>{
        "name"=>"d72374bco5g9u4s4f9e06e8e6014bdfdf",
        "hostname"=>"10.0.36.89",
```

```
        "host"=>"10.0.36.89",
        "port"=>3306,
        "user"=>"uroCGNAJpmoK6",
        "username"=>"uroCGNAJpmoK6",
        "password"=>"p4gGbogusJ7Il"
      }
    }
  ]
}
```

The code must perform the following steps:

1. Read the variable.

2. Parse it into the data structure.

3. The data structure is a hash of arrays. Extract the value whose key is `mysql-5.1`, since this is the array of MySQL services.

4. Each array element is a hash of data for a specific service. Find the element that contains a `name` key with a value that matches the service we want.

5. This hash contains a key `credentials` whose value is a hash containing the credentials we need. Extract it.

These steps are easier to express in Ruby than in English. If the name of the service is `insideaf-mysql` then this is the code that extracts the credentials:

```
creds = (JSON.parse(ENV['VCAP_SERVICES']))['mysql-5.1'].each do |s|
  break(s) if s['name'] == 'insideaf-mysql'
end)['credentials']
```

Next we use the credentials to connect to the database:

```
client = Mysql2::Client.new(:host => creds['host'],
    :username => creds['user'],
    :password => creds['password'], :database => creds['name'],
    :host => creds['host'], :port => creds['port'])
```

Finally, we need to change the code that responds to the page request. The old version looks like the following code:

```
get '/' do
  @env = ENV
  erb :index
end
```

In the new version, the instance variable is set to the results variable for a database query:

```
get '/' do
  @rows = client.query('select * from Tasks', :cast_booleans => true)
  erb :index
end
```

The following code is the entire source file in one place:

```
require 'sinatra'
require 'json'
require 'mysql2'
creds = (JSON.parse(ENV['VCAP_SERVICES'])['mysql-5.1'].each do |s|
  break(s) if s['name'] == 'insideaf-mysql'
end)['credentials']
client = Mysql2::Client.new(:host => creds['host'],
    :username => creds['user'],
    :password => creds['password'], :database => creds['name'],
    :host => creds['host'], :port => creds['port'])
get '/' do
  @rows = client.query('select * from Tasks', :cast_booleans => true)
  erb :index
end
```

Changes to views/index.erb

Changes to the template file are a matter of descriptive text and variable references. Here's the old version:

```
<html><head>
  <title>Environment Variables</title>
</head><body>
  <h1>Environment Variables</h2>
  <table border="1" cellpadding="5">
    <tr>
      <td>Name</td>
      <td>Value</td>
    </tr>
    <% @env.each do |name, value| %>
      <% value = value[0..19] + "..." if value.length > 20 %>
      <tr>
        <td><%= name %></td>
        <td><%= value %></td>
```

```
        </tr>
      <% end %>
    </table>
  </body>
  </html>
```

And the new version is as follows:

```
<html><head>
  <title>Tasks</title>
</head><body>
  <h1>Tasks</h1>
  <table border="1" cellpadding="5">
    <tr>
      <td>Name</td>
      <td>Completed</td>
    </tr>
    <% @rows.each do |row| %>
      <tr>
        <td><%= row['Name'] %></td>
        <td><%= row['Completed'] %></td>
      </tr>
    <% end %>
  </table>
</body></html>
```

Changing Gemfile

As we've added new Gems to this project, we need to change part of the overall
project configuration. This is contained in Gemfile, a simple list of Gems used in
the project. The old version is as follows:

```
source :rubygems

gem "sinatra"
gem "thin"
```

The first line indicates a standard server for downloading Gems. This server has
been deprecated for security reasons, so we'll change it in a moment.

Notice that Gemfile contains a line for the Sinatra Gem, which we referenced in the
application, and an additional Gem, thin. This is a simple web server used by the
Sinatra framework.

The modified Gemfile incorporates new Gems and a safer source:

```
source 'http://rubygems.org'

gem "sinatra"
gem "thin"
gem "json"
gem "mysql2"
```

When you modify Gemfile, you must incorporate changes using the following command:

```
bundle install
```

If you do not have "bundle" installed, you will have to install that gem before running bundle install. To do this, simply run the following command:

```
sudo gem install bundler
```

The AppFog requires this command in order to detect the Gems it must provide for you. The command also installs gems locally so that your local Gem set matches the one you're using on AppFog.

Once again update the AppFog version using the following command:

```
af update insideaf2
```

And you now have a database listing on the live site as shown in the following screenshot:

Summary

In this chapter we created an application from scratch that used one of AppFog's database services. The steps we took were as follows:

1. Configure one of AppFog's standard applications to manage our database.
2. Create a MySQL database including creating a simple table with sample data.
3. Create a new application that will use the database.

In the next chapter we will create an application from scratch using AppFog's command line interface.

4
Creating an Application from Scratch

The AppFog console is a very useful tool, but you can also create applications completely from the command line. In this chapter, we will create a simple application directly from the command line and publish it as a new application to AppFog.

Creating an application

We could use the application we created and downloaded in *Chapter 2, Using the Command Line Tool*, however we are going to create a very new application. This application is also going to be a Sinatra application that displays some basic date and time information.

First, navigate to a new directory that will be used to contain the code. Everything in this directory will be uploaded to AppFog when we create the new application.

```
$ mkdir insideaf4
$ cd insideaf4
```

Now, create a new file called insideaf4.rb. The contents of the file should look like the following:

```
require 'sinatra'

get '/' do
  erb :index
end
```

As we saw in the previous chapter, this tells Sinatra to listen for requests to the base URL of / and then render the index page that we will create next.

If you are using Ruby 1.8.7, you may need to add the following line at the top, as described in *Chapter 2, Using the Command Line Tool*:

```
require 'rubygems'
```

Next, create a new directory called views under the insideaf4 directory:

```
$ mkdir views
$ cd views
```

Now we are going to create a new file under the views directory called index.erb. This file will be the one that displays the date and time information for our example.

The following are the contents of the index.erb file:

```
<html><head>
  <title>Current Time</title>
</head><body>
  <% time = Time.new %>
  <h1>Current Time</h1>
  <table border="1" cellpadding="5">
    <tr>
      <td>Name</td>
      <td>Value</td>
    </tr>
    <tr>
      <td>Date (M/D/Y)</td>
      <td<%= time.strftime('%m/%d/%Y') %></td>
    </tr>
    <tr>
      <td>Time</td>
      <td><%= time.strftime('%I:%M %p') %></td>
    </tr>
    <tr>
      <td>Month</td>
      <td><%= time.strftime('%B') %></td>
    </tr>
    <tr>
      <td>Day</td>
      <td><%= time.strftime('%A') %></td>
    </tr>
  </table>
</body></html>
```

This file will create a table that shows a number of different ways to format the date and time. Embedded in the HTML code are Ruby snippets that look like `<%= %>`. Inside of these snippets we use Ruby's `strftime` method to display the current date and time in a number of different string formats. At the beginning of the file, we create a new instance of a `Time` object which is automatically set to the current time. Then we use the `strftime` method to display different values in the table.

For more information on using Ruby dates, please see the documentation available at `http://www.ruby-doc.org/core-2.0.0/Time.html`.

Testing the application

Before creating an application in AppFog, it is useful to test it out locally first. To do this you will again need the Sinatra Gem installed. If you need to do that, refer to *Appendix, Installing the AppFog Gem*.

The following is the command to run your small application:

```
$ ruby indiseaf4.rb
```

You will see the Sinatra application start and then you can navigate to `http://localhost:4567/` in a browser. You should see a page that has the current date and time information like the following screenshot:

Current Time

Name	Value
Date (M/D/Y)	10/15/2013
Time	08:26 PM
Month	October
Day	Tuesday

To terminate the application, return to the command line and press *Control+C*.

Publishing to AppFog

Now that you have a working application, you can publish it to AppFog and create the new AppFog application.

Before you begin, make sure you are in the root director of your project. For this example that was the `insideaf4` directory.

Next, you will need to log in to AppFog.

```
$ af login
Attempting login to [https://api.appfog.com]
Email: matt@somecompany.com
Password: ********
Successfully logged into [https://api.appfog.com]
```

You may be asked for your e-mail and password again, but the tool may remember your session if you logged in recently.

Now you can push your application to AppFog, which will create a new application for you. Make sure you are in the correct directory and use the `Push` command. You will be prompted for a number of settings during the publishing process. In each case there will be a list of options along with a default. The default value will be listed with a capital letter or listed by itself in square brackets. For our purposes, you can just press *Enter* for each prompt to accept the default value. The only exception to that is the step that prompts you to choose an infrastructure. In that step you will need to make a selection.

```
$ af push insideaf4
Would you like to deploy from the current directory? [Yn]:
Detected a Sinatra Application, is this correct? [Yn]:
1: AWS US East - Virginia
2: AWS EU West - Ireland
3: AWS Asia SE - Singapore
4: HP AZ 2 - Las Vegas
Select Infrastructure:
Application Deployed URL [insideaf4.aws.af.cm]:
Memory reservation (128M, 256M, 512M, 1G, 2G) [128M]:
How many instances? [1]:
Bind existing services to insideaf4? [yN]:
Create services to bind to insideaf4? [yN]:
Would you like to save this configuration? [yN]:
Creating Application: OK
Uploading Application:
  Checking for available resources: OK
```

```
   Packing application: OK
   Uploading (1K): OK
Push Status: OK
Staging Application insideaf4: OK
Starting Application insideaf4: OK
```

Command-line options

You can accept the default values during the push and you will get a valid application deployed. However, if you wanted to change something, the following command-line options are explained.

```
Would you like to deploy from the current directory? [Yn]:
```

The default is yes. If you type n for no, then you will be prompted for the deployment path. The path is relative to your current directory. One way to tell if you enter a path that does not exist is that you will be asked to enter a number of questions manually, such as the application type and runtime environment.

```
Detected a Sinatra Application, is this correct? [Yn]:
```

If you choose no, then you will be presented with a list of application types. It is a numbered list so you will just need to find the correct type and enter the number. The list of options includes Grails, Standalone, Node, Sinatra, PHP, Rails, and many others.

```
1: AWS US East - Virginia
2: AWS EU West - Ireland
3: AWS Asia SE - Singapore
4: HP AZ 2 - Las Vegas
Select Infrastructure:
```

This step lets you choose where to host your application. Typically you can choose a location that is close to your users. For this example I will choose 1 for the United States location.

```
Application Deployed URL [insideaf4.aws.af.cm]:
```

You can choose any available URL. If you are using the free plan, then you must ensure the URL ends with aws.af.cm, otherwise you will get an error that External URIs are not enabled for this account.

```
Memory reservation (128M, 256M, 512M, 1G, 2G) [128M]:
```

If you need to allocate more memory to your app, then you can choose one of the other options. If you try to allocate more memory than you have available, you will get an error that says you have exceeded your available memory.

```
How many instances? [1]:
```

You can select the number of available instances of your application you want to be running. Like with memory, if you try to configure more instances than available, you will get an error.

```
Bind existing services to insideaf4? [yN]:
```

If you want to use an existing service, you can enter yes to this prompt. You will be provided with a list of existing services as a numbered list. Enter the number of the service you would like to use with this application.

```
Create services to bind to insideaf4? [yN]:
```

If you need to create a service, enter y here. You will be presented with a list of possible services to choose from, such as mongodb, mysql, rabbitmq. Once you choose a type, you will be prompted for a name. You will then be asked if you want to create more services, which allows you to create as many services as needed.

```
Would you like to save this configuration? [yN]:
```

The last prompt is to save the configuration if desired. If you choose to save the configuration, a new manifest.yml file will be written to your current directory. This file can be used as a reference to what configuration options were used when creating an application. For more information on the manifest files, you can read the AppFog documentation on the subject available at https://docs.appfog.com/getting-started/af-cli/manifests.

Testing the published application

To test out the running application, you can point your browser to the new URL. In the above example, you would go to http://insideaf4.aws.af.cm. You should see the same **Current Time** page you saw when running locally.

Another way to make sure you application is running is to use the command line:

```
$ af apps
+-------------+---+---------+----------------------+----------+-----+
| Application | # | Health  | URLS                 | Services | In  |
+-------------+---+---------+----------------------+----------+-----+
| insideaf4   | 1 | RUNNING | insideaf4.aws.af.cm  |          | aws |
+-------------+---+---------+----------------------+----------+-----+
```

This will list all of your installed applications.

Managing the published application

Now that you have an application published, there are a few more things you can do from the command line to manage the application. A more in-depth list of command line options will be discussed in *Chapter 5, Command-line Reference.*

To see a list of all the uploaded files:

```
$ af files insideaf4
app/                                              -
logs/                                             -
```

You can navigate inside of the directories using a command like the following:

```
$ af files insideaf4 app/
insideaf4.rb                              52B
views/                                    -
$ af files insideaf4 app/views/
index.erb                                 600B
```

To restart, stop, or start the application use the following command:

```
$ af restart insideaf4
Stopping Application 'insideaf4': OK
Staging Application 'insideaf4': OK
Starting Application 'insideaf4': OK
$ af stop insideaf4
Stopping Application 'insideaf4': OK
$ af start insideaf4
Staging Application 'insideaf4': OK
Starting Application 'insideaf4': OK
```

If you want to view the logs for your application, you can see the last few lines of the stderr.log and stdout.log files using this command:

```
$ af logs insideaf4
====> /logs/stderr.log <====


== Sinatra/1.3.2 has taken the stage on 50566 for production with backup
from Th
```

```
in
76.113.232.68, 127.0.0.1 - - [16/Oct/2013 02:05:00] "GET / HTTP/1.1" 200
497 0.0
075


====> /logs/stdout.log <====


>> Thin web server (v1.3.1 codename Triple Espresso)
>> Maximum connections set to 1024
>> Listening on 0.0.0.0:50566, CTRL+C to stop
```

If you want to see details like uptime, CPU utilization, memory use, and disk space used, you can use the `stats` command. This will display the statistics for each instance of the application you have running:

```
$ af stats insideaf4
+--------+-----------+---------------+------------+-----------+
|Instance|CPU (Cores)|Memory (limit)|Disk (limit)|Uptime     |
+--------+-----------+---------------+------------+-----------+
|0       |0.3% (2)   |22.2M (128M)  |0B (1G)     |0d:0h:5m:20s|
+--------+-----------+---------------+------------+-----------+
```

Finally, if you want to delete the application you can use the following command. However, be cautious because there is no confirmation asking if you are sure, and this will permanently delete your application.

```
$af delete insideaf4
Deleting application [insideaf4]: OK
```

Summary

In this chapter we created an application from scratch which involved:

- Creating a Sinatra and Ruby application
- Testing the application locally
- Uploading the application to AppFog and testing it
- Managing the application using the AppFog command line.

In *Chapter 5, Command-line Reference* we are going to learn more uses of the AppFog command line tool.

5

Command-line Reference

In *Chapter 2, Using the Command-line Tool*, you used the command line tool to pull down an application created in AppFog. In *Chapter 4, Creating an Application from Scratch*, you used the command line tool to create an application from scratch.

In this chapter we are going to learn more about the various command line options. For each group of commands, we will list the commands in that group and then give some examples of their use.

Finding help

To start, there are two commands you can use to find more information about all the commands listed in this chapter.

Command	Description
af help [command]	Without any command, this will list all the possible commands. When you supply a parameter, this will give details about the usage for that command.
af help options	Lists options that are used for various commands. For example, you can use --verbose for more detailed output.

By typing just af help, you will get a list of all the available commands. These commands will be explained later in this chapter.

```
Start Command Prompt with Ruby

C:\>af help

Usage: af [options] command [<args>] [command_options]
Try 'af help [command]' or 'af help options' for more information.

Currently available af commands are:

  Getting Started
    target [url]                          Reports current target or sets a new target
    login  [email] [--email, --passwd]    Login
    info                                  System and account information

  Applications
    apps                                  List deployed applications

  Application Creation
    push [appname]                        Create, push, map, and start a new applicati
    push [appname] --infra                Push application to specified infrastructure
    push [appname] --path                 Push application from specified path
    push [appname] --url                  Set the url for the application
    push [appname] --instances <N>        Set the expected number <N> of instances
    push [appname] --mem M                Set the memory reservation for the applicati
    push [appname] --runtime RUNTIME      Set the runtime to use for the application
    push [appname] --debug [MODE]         Push application and start in a debug mode
    push [appname] --no-start             Do not auto-start the application

  Application Operations
    start <appname> [--debug [MODE]]      Start the application
    stop  <appname>                       Stop the application
    restart <appname> [--debug [MODE]]    Restart the application
    delete <appname>                      Delete the application
    clone <src-app> <dest-app> [infra]    Clone the application and services

  Application Updates
    update <appname> [--path,--debug [MODE]]  Update the application bits
    mem <appname> [memsize]               Update the memory reservation for an applica
    map <appname> <url>                   Register the application to the url
    unmap <appname> <url>                 Unregister the application from the url
    instances <appname> <num|delta>      Scale the application instances up or down

  Application Information
    crashes <appname>                     List recent application crashes
    crashlogs <appname>                   Display log information for crashed applicat
```

If you want more information about one command, you can pass along the name of the command to get usage details. For example:

```
$ af help login
```

Getting account information

These commands give you information about your account, and are independent of any one application.

Command	Description
`af login [email] [--email EMAIL, --passwd PASSWORD]`	Login to your AppFog account. You can pass your e-mail, which will prompt you for a password, or you can pass both your e-mail and password. If you do not supply either your e-mail or your password you will be prompted for them. See further for examples.
`af logout`	Log out of your account.
`af info`	Provides details about your account such as how much used and available memory, services, and apps you have.
`af apps`	List your current apps. See previous chapters for examples.
`af user`	Display your currently logged in e-mail address/user name.
`af passwd`	Change your password. Note that this is different from user as it actually changes your password and does not just display your password.
`af targets`	Display a list of possible API targets and your authorization token.
`af target [url]`	Change your API target URL.

There are a number of different ways you can use the `af login` command. Which one you use depends on how much information you want to provide on the command line, and how much you want to manually enter. If you are using a script, you may want to pass both e-mail and password on the command line; however that will expose your password in plain text. Here are the different ways to enter the command:

```
$ af login
Attempting login to [https://api.appfog.com]
Email: matt@somecompany.com
Password: ********
Successfully logged into [https://api.appfog.com]


$ af login matt@somecompany.com
Attempting login to [https://api.appfog.com]
Password: ********
Successfully logged into [https://api.appfog.com]


$ af login --email matt@somecompany.com --passwd mypassword
Attempting login to [https://api.appfog.com]
Successfully logged into [https://api.appfog.com]
```

Another interesting command to point out is the `af info` command. This will give you statistics for your account. This will tell you how much memory you are using out of your allocated amount, how many services you have configured, and how many apps you have installed. The following is an example of the output:

```
$ af info


AppFog Free Your Cloud Edition
For support visit http://support.appfog.com


Target:    https://api.appfog.com (v0.999)
Client:    v0.3.18.12


User:      matt@somecompany.com
Usage:     Memory    (1.1G of 2.0G total)
           Services (1 of 8 total)
           Apps      (2 of 9999 total)
```

Creating and updating an application

The following commands are used to create, update, and delete your application:

Command	Description
`af push [appname]`	Creates a new application. See *Chapter 4, Creating an Application from Scratch*, for more details. There are a number of command-line options you can use along with this command to set default values. Use `af help push` for more details.
`af update [appname]`	Uploads a new version of the application code to the AppFog cloud. You can use the `--path` option to point to the location of the code. See further for an example.
`af delete [appname]`	Deletes the application from AppFog. The tool will not ask for any confirmation, so using this command will immediately delete your application.
`af clone [src-app] [dest-app] [infra]`	Creates a copy of an existing application. See further for an example.
`af runtimes`	Sees which versions of the different runtimes are currently supported. The runtimes include Ruby, Java, PHP, and more.
`af frameworks`	Sees a list of supported frameworks. Frameworks are applications, such as Sinatra, Rails, Grails, and more.
`af infras`	Sees a list of supported infrastructures, such as AWS US East and AWS EU West.

In *Chapter 4, Creating an Application from Scratch*, we showed examples of how to use `af push` to create an application and the `af delete` command to delete an application.

To update the new version of the application you use the `af update` command. There are two ways to update your application. First is from within the application directory, where you can use the `af update` command directly. If you are in a different directory, you can use the `--path` option to point to your directory. When using the path attribute, it works best if you use the full path to your application directory. The following are examples of each usage:

```
$ af update insideaf4
Uploading Application:
  Checking for available resources: OK
  Packing application: OK
```

```
  Uploading (1K): OK
Push Status: OK
Stopping Application 'insideaf4': OK
Staging Application 'insideaf4': OK
Starting Application 'insideaf4': OK


$ af update insideaf4 --path /code/insideaf4
Uploading Application:
  Checking for available resources: OK
  Packing application: OK
  Uploading (1K): OK
Push Status: OK
Stopping Application 'insideaf4': OK
Staging Application 'insideaf4': OK
Starting Application 'insideaf4': OK
```

To make a copy of an existing application, you can use the `af clone` command. If you do not pass a specific infrastructure to the command, you will be prompted for it. To get a list of available infrastructures, use the `af infras` command.

```
$ af clone insideaf4 insideaf5
1: AWS US East - Virginia
2: AWS EU West - Ireland
3: AWS Asia SE - Singapore
4: HP AZ 2 - Las Vegas
Select Infrastructure: 1
Application Deployed URL [insideaf5.aws.af.cm]:
Pulling last pushed source code: OK
Cloning 'insideaf4' to 'insideaf5':
Uploading Application:
  Checking for available resources: OK
  Packing application: OK
  Uploading (1K): OK
Push Status: OK
```

```
Staging Application 'insideaf5': OK

Starting Application 'insideaf5': OK

$ af clone insideaf4 insideaf6 aws

Application Deployed URL [insideaf6.aws.af.cm]:

Pulling last pushed source code: OK

Cloning 'insideaf4' to 'insideaf6':

Uploading Application:

  Checking for available resources: OK

  Packing application: OK

  Uploading (1K): OK

Push Status: OK

Staging Application 'insideaf6': OK

Starting Application 'insideaf6': OK
```

Gathering application information

There are a number of commands you can use to find information about your currently installed applications.

Command	Description
af logs [appname]	Displays log files for the application. See *Chapter 4, Creating an Application from Scratch*, for examples.
af files [appname] [path]	Lists the files for an application. Add a path to navigate through the remote file system. See *Chapter 4, Creating an Application from Scratch*, for examples.
af stats [appname]	Displays stats for an application like uptime, CPU utilization, memory use, and disk space used. See *Chapter 4, Creating an Application from Scratch*, for examples.
af crashes [appname]	Lists any crashes for a given application.
af crashlogs [appname]	Displays crash logs, for example stderr.log, for an application.

If you are experiencing problems with your application, these commands can be very helpful. For example, you can see information about recent crashes using the `af crashes` and `af crashlogs` commands. If you want to see your logging output, you can use `af logs`. If you want to verify what files are deployed, you can use `af files`. See *Chapter 4, Creating an Application from Scratch*, for examples of the usage of these commands.

Managing your application

These commands can be used to control and configure your application.

Command	Description
`af start [appname]`	Starts an application.
`af stop [appname]`	Stops an application.
`af restart [appname]`	Restarts an application.
`af mem [appname] [memsize]`	Updates the amount of memory allocated for your application.
`af map [appname] [url]`	Maps an application to a given URL.
`af unmap [appname] [url]`	Removes an application from a given URL.
`af instances [appname]`	Displays the configured instances of an application along with state (for example, RUNNING) and start time for each one.
`af instances [appname] [num]`	Changes the number of configured instances.
`af env [appname]`	Lists custom environment variables for an application.
`af env-add [appname] [variable=value]`	Adds an environment variable specific to an application.
`af env-del [appname] [variable]`	Removes an environment variable for an application.

The basic commands to start, stop, and restart are described in more detail in *Chapter 4, Creating an Application from Scratch*.

If you want to change the configuration of your application, the other commands are useful. First, the following shows how to change the number of running instances you have for your application:

```
$ af instances insideaf4

+-------+---------+--------------------+
| Index | State   | Start Time         |
+-------+---------+--------------------+
| 0     | RUNNING | 10/21/2013 09:18PM |
+-------+---------+--------------------+


$ af instances insideaf4 2
Scaling Application instances up to 2: OK


$ af instances insideaf4

+-------+---------+--------------------+
| Index | State   | Start Time         |
+-------+---------+--------------------+
| 0     | RUNNING | 10/21/2013 09:18PM |
| 1     | RUNNING | 10/21/2013 09:35PM |
+-------+---------+--------------------+
```

Next, here is how to change the amount of allocated memory. The first example will prompt you for how much memory to allocate. The second example will pass the memory allocation with the command:

```
$ af mem insideaf4
Update Memory Reservation? (64M, 128M, 256M, 512M) [128M]: 256M
Updating Memory Reservation to 256M: OK
Stopping Application 'insideaf4': OK
Staging Application 'insideaf4': OK
Starting Application 'insideaf4': OK
```

```
$ af mem insideaf4 128M
Updating Memory Reservation to 128M: OK
Stopping Application 'insideaf4': OK
Staging Application 'insideaf4': OK
Starting Application 'insideaf4': OK
```

If you need to use environment variables, you can use the different env commands. The following is a series of commands to add a new environment variable and then later remove it:

```
$ af env insideaf4
No Environment Variables


$ af env-add insideaf4 debug=true
Adding Environment Variable [debug=true]: OK
Stopping Application 'insideaf4': OK
Staging Application 'insideaf4': OK
Starting Application 'insideaf4': OK


$ af env insideaf4
+----------+-------+
| Variable | Value |
+----------+-------+
| debug    | true  |
+----------+-------+


$ af env-del insideaf4 debug
Deleting Environment Variable [debug]: OK
Stopping Application 'insideaf4': OK
Staging Application 'insideaf4': OK
Starting Application 'insideaf4': OK


$ af env insideaf4
No Environment Variables
```

Another configuration you may want to change is the URL to which your application is mapped. You can use the `af apps` command to see the current URLs, and the `af map` and `af unmap` commands to add and remove URLs in the following way.

 The `af apps` output has been condensed in these examples.

```
$ af apps
+-------------+----------------------+
| Application | URLS                 |
+-------------+----------------------+
| insideaf4   | insideaf4.aws.af.cm  |
+-------------+----------------------+


$ af map insideaf4 insideaf5.aws.af.cm
Successfully mapped url


$ af apps
+-------------+---------------------------------------------+
| Application | URLS                                        |
+-------------+---------------------------------------------+
| insideaf4   | insideaf4.aws.af.cm, insideaf5.aws.af.cm    |
+-------------+---------------------------------------------+


$ af unmap insideaf4 insideaf5.aws.af.cm
Successfully unmapped url
```

Using services

Use the command line to create and manage services such as remote databases.

Command	Description
`af services`	Lists available and configured services for your account.
`af create-service [service]`	Creates a new service. You will be prompted for the type (if not passed as parameter) and name of the service.
`af delete-service [servicename]`	Removes a service. If you do not provide a service name, you will be presented with a list of all of your services.
`af bind-service [servicename] [appname]`	Associates a service with an application.
`af unbind-service [servicename] [appname]`	Removes the association of a service with an application.
`af clone-services [sourceapp] [destingationapp]`	Clones all the services from one app to another one.
`af tunnel`	Creates a tunnel to a remote service. For example, this is useful to query your remote databases. Using this command requires the `caldecott gem`.

Often it will be easier to create services from the AppFog web console. However, it is possible to do it from the command line as well. In this example, we will create a new MySQL database service and associate it with an existing application. It is important to note that when deleting a service with the command line, you will not be prompted to confirm the deletion, so be sure you use the correct command:

```
$ af create-service mysql insideaf4-db
1: AWS US East - Virginia
2: AWS EU West - Ireland
3: AWS Asia SE - Singapore
4: HP AZ 2 - Las Vegas
Select Infrastructure: 1
Creating Service: OK

$ af bind-service insideaf4-db insideaf4
Binding Service [insideaf4-db]: OK
Stopping Application 'insideaf4': OK
```

```
Staging Application 'insideaf4': OK
Starting Application 'insideaf4': OK


$ af services


============== System Services ==============


+------------+---------+-----------------------------+
| Service    | Version | Description                 |
+------------+---------+-----------------------------+
| mongodb    | 1.8     | MongoDB NoSQL store         |
| mysql      | 5.1     | MySQL database service      |
| postgresql | 9.1     | PostgreSQL database service |
| rabbitmq   | 2.4     | RabbitMQ message queue      |
| redis      | 2.2     | Redis key-value store service |
+------------+---------+-----------------------------+


=========== Provisioned Services ============


+--------------+---------+-----+
| Name         | Service | In  |
+--------------+---------+-----+
| insideaf4-db | mysql   | aws |
+--------------+---------+-----+


$ af apps


+-------------+--------------+
| Application | Services     |
+-------------+--------------+
| insideaf4   | insideaf4-db |
+-------------+--------------+


$ af unbind-service insideaf4-db insideaf4
Unbinding Service [insideaf4-db]: OK
Stopping Application 'insideaf4': OK
```

```
Staging Application 'insideaf4': OK

Starting Application 'insideaf4': OK


$ af delete-service insideaf4-db

Deleting service [insideaf4-db]: OK
```

Creating aliases

You can use aliases to map a command to a custom command that is easier to remember or shorter to type.

Command	Description
af alias [alias=command]	Creates an alias.
af aliases	Lists all of the aliases you have set up.
af unalias [alias]	Removes an alias you had previously configured.

Using aliases is currently fairly restricted. For example, you cannot create an alias that includes parameters. However, if you just want to change the command name, following is an example. In this example we will create an alias to use lo instead of logout:

```
$af aliases
No Aliases


$ af alias lo=logout
Successfully aliased 'lo' to 'logout'


$ af aliases
+-------+---------+
| Alias | Command |
+-------+---------+
| lo    | logout  |
+-------+---------+


$ af lo
Successfully logged out of [https://api.appfog.com]


$ af unalias lo
Successfully unaliased 'lo'
```

Summary

In this chapter we learned how to use the AppFog command line by listing out the commands and showing examples of many of the important commands. If you want more information, you can use the `af help` command or see the documentation online available at `https://docs.appfog.com/getting-started/af-cli`.

Installing the AppFog Gem

The AppFog command line tool is implemented using Ruby, so you need to install it as a Ruby Gem. That also means you must have Ruby installed in order to use the command line tool.

In Ruby, a Gem is a way to package and distribute programs and libraries.

This appendix gives instructions for installing Ruby and the AppFog Gem on various common platforms. The Ruby packages described are those easily installed, except on Macintosh, where Ruby 1.8.7 is preinstalled. These versions of Ruby are not typically used for serious Ruby development, but are adequate for running the AppFog command line tool.

If you are interested in Ruby development, see the last section, *The Ruby Version Manager*. In addition to the AppFog Gem, you will also need the Sinatra Gem to use with the examples in this book. Sinatra is a free and simple web application framework built on top of Ruby. You can find out more information about Sinatra at http://www.sinatrarb.com.

Installing on Macintosh

OS X comes with Ruby 1.8.7 preinstalled. This version is rapidly falling out of use by the Ruby development community, but it does support the AppFog Gem. If your sole use of Ruby is to work with AppFog, you don't need to install a later version of Ruby. If you do plan to do Ruby application development, consider installing RVM. See the section *The Ruby Version Manager*.

You'll use the sudo command to install the AppFog Gem. This command requires that you have a non-blank administrator password. For more information, refer to *Mac OS X: sudo command requires a non-blank admin password* available at http://support.apple.com/kb/HT4103.

To install the AppFog Gem, open a Terminal window, and enter the following two commands:

```
sudo gem install af
sudo gem install sinatra
```

Installing on CentOS

On CentOS, you need superuser privileges to install a software package. The simplest way to do this is to enter superuser mode using the su command.

1. Enter superuser mode

    ```
    $ su -
    #
    ```

2. Install the basic Ruby package. Type yes as prompted.

    ```
    # yum install ruby
    ```

3. Install Ruby packages for development and documentation.

    ```
    # yum install ruby-devel ruby-irb ruby-rdoc ruby-ri
    ```

4. Install the Rubygems package.

    ```
    # yum install rubygems
    ```

5. Install the AppFog gem.

    ```
    # gem install af
    ```

6. Install the AppFog gem.

    ```
    # gem install af
    ```

7. Install the Sinatra gem.

    ```
    # gem install sinatra
    ```

8. Exit superuser mode.

    ```
    # exit
    $
    ```

Always exit the superuser mode after installing the software. Doing routine tasks as superuser is likely to cause security and other problems.

You will need to re-enter the superuser mode to install Gems, including the AppFog command line tool.

You can use the `sudo` tool to enter single commands as superuser. On CentOS this feature is not enabled by default. Refer to the system documentation for more information.

Installing on Ubuntu

On Ubuntu, you need superuser privileges to install software. To run a command with superuser privileges, precede it with `sudo`.

1. Install the Ruby package.

    ```
    sudo apt-get install ruby1.9.1
    ```

2. Install the AppFog gem

    ```
    sudo gem install af
    ```

3. Install the Sinatra gem

    ```
    sudo gem install af
    ```

The `sudo` command works for users with administrator status. The first user created when Ubuntu is installed automatically gets administrator status.

Installing on Windows

1. Go to the RubyInstaller download page available at
    `http://rubyinstaller.org/downloads/`.

2. Choose and download the latest installer from the list. All the provided
    installers support the AppFog command line.

 You can use a 64-bit version of Ruby (marked x64) if you are
sure you have a 64-bit version of Windows. If you have a 32-bit
version of Windows, or are unsure, download one of the other
installers, which work on both 32-bit and 64-bit Windows.

3. Run the downloaded installer. If you are running a recent version of
    Windows, a **Security Warning** dialog will appear; confirm that the
    program has your permission to run.

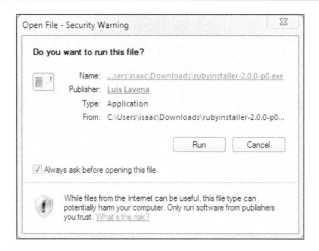

4. A sequence of dialogs appears. These allow you to specify installation language and agree to licensing terms. The configuration dialog is crucial.

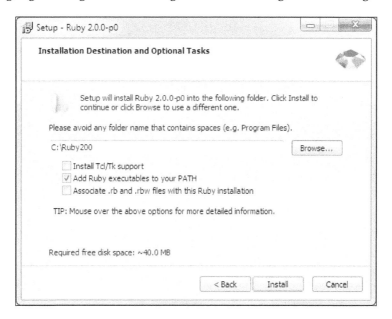

5. Be sure that **Add Ruby executables to your PATH** is checked. You can also install Tcl/Tk support and associate source files, but these are not needed for AppFog.

6. Once Ruby is installed, a new program group appears in the Start Menu under **All Programs**.

7. The shortcut **Start Command Prompt with Ruby** opens a command line window with the correct settings for using Ruby. Use this shortcut for all AppFog command line actions. You may want to copy it to the desktop or pin it to the status bar.

8. Use the command line to install the AppFog Gem.

```
c:\Users\isaac>gem install af
```

9. Use the command line to install the Sinatra gem.

```
c:\Users\isaac>gem install sinatra
```

Using the Ruby Version Manager

Ruby Version Manager (**RVM**) is a tool for managing Ruby installation on UNIX (including OS X) and Linux. This probably raises two questions in your mind: Why not just install Ruby directly? And if RVM is important, why doesn't this book say more about it?

RVM has two benefits that you don't get when installing Ruby directly:

1. It allows you to work with multiple versions of Ruby on the same machine. This makes it easier to deal with issues relating to a rapidly evolving language.

2. It helps you identify non-Ruby dependencies in your Gems.

These features are important to Ruby developers, but not to users who simply need access to the Ruby Gem that implements the AppFog command line tool. Because this book isn't about Ruby programming and because working with RVM can get very complicated, we won't cover RVM installation or use.

If you're interested in RVM, you can visit the website `https://rvm.io/`.

Index

S

services
 creating, commands used 58
Sinatra
 URL 63
Sinatra application
 creating 39-41
 publishing, to AppFog 41
 testing 41
su command 64
sudo command 63, 65

U

Ubuntu
 AppFog Gem, installing on 65

V

views
 modifying 34

W

Windows
 AppFog Gem, installing on 66-68

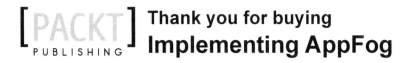
Thank you for buying
Implementing AppFog

About Packt Publishing

Packt, pronounced 'packed', published its first book "*Mastering phpMyAdmin for Effective MySQL Management*" in April 2004 and subsequently continued to specialize in publishing highly focused books on specific technologies and solutions.

Our books and publications share the experiences of your fellow IT professionals in adapting and customizing today's systems, applications, and frameworks. Our solution based books give you the knowledge and power to customize the software and technologies you're using to get the job done. Packt books are more specific and less general than the IT books you have seen in the past. Our unique business model allows us to bring you more focused information, giving you more of what you need to know, and less of what you don't.

Packt is a modern, yet unique publishing company, which focuses on producing quality, cutting-edge books for communities of developers, administrators, and newbies alike. For more information, please visit our website: www.packtpub.com.

Writing for Packt

We welcome all inquiries from people who are interested in authoring. Book proposals should be sent to author@packtpub.com. If your book idea is still at an early stage and you would like to discuss it first before writing a formal book proposal, contact us; one of our commissioning editors will get in touch with you.

We're not just looking for published authors; if you have strong technical skills but no writing experience, our experienced editors can help you develop a writing career, or simply get some additional reward for your expertise.

Instant AppFog [Instant]

ISBN: 978-1-78216-762-4 Paperback: 58 pages

A practical guide to getting started with AppFog to deploy and manage your apps

1. Learn something new in an Instant! A short, fast, focused guide delivering immediate results

2. Deploy and manage your applications on AppFog easily using the AppFog tools and web console

3. Secure your application using SSL on AppFog

Instant CakePHP Starter [Instant]

ISBN: 978-1-78216-260-5 Paperback: 76 pages

Learn everything you need to develop a feature-rich CakePHP app, from installation to deployement

1. Learn something new in an Instant! A short, fast, focused guide delivering immediate results

2. Focus on an iterative practical approach to learn the myriad features of CakePHP

3. Learn about Models, Views, and Controllers as well as scaffolding, themes, behaviors, and routing

4. Scaffold and generate your application code using the command-line "bake" tool almost exclusively

Please check **www.PacktPub.com** for information on our titles

CakePHP Application Development

ISBN: 978-1-84719-389-6   Paperback: 332 pages

Step-by-step introduction to rapid web developement using the open-source MVC CakePHP framework

1. Develop cutting-edge Web 2.0 applications, and write PHP code in a faster, more productive way

2. Walk through the creation of a complete CakePHP Web application

3. Customize the look and feel of applications using CakePHP layouts and views

OpenCV 2 Computer Vision Application Programming Cookbook

ISBN: 978-1-84951-324-1   Paperback: 304 pages

Over 50 recipes to master this library of programming functions for real-time computer vision

1. Teaches you how to program computer vision applications in C++ using the different features of the OpenCV library

2. Demonstrates the important structures and functions of OpenCV in detail with complete working examples

3. Describes fundamental concepts in computer vision and image processing

Please check **www.PacktPub.com** for information on our titles

www.ingramcontent.com/pod-product-compliance
Lightning Source LLC
LaVergne TN
LVHW080103070326
832902LV00014B/2393